Word Wise

Scott Foresman
Practice Station Flip Chart

Reading STREET

Grade 3

ISBN-13: 978-0-328-53719-8
ISBN-10: 0-328-53719-5

EAN

9 780328 537198

9000

ISBN-13: 978-328-53719-8
ISBN-10:   328-53719-5
9 10 V0B4 14

Word Wise

Short Vowels; Syllables VC/CV

15 min.

You will need

- Teacher-made word cards
- Letter Tiles
- paper
- pencils

● Choose eight word cards from those provided by your teacher. Use the Letter Tiles to spell the words. Write sentences using four of the words.

▲ Choose eight word cards from those provided by your teacher. Use the Letter Tiles to spell the words. Write sentences using the words.

■ Choose ten word cards from those provided by your teacher. Write the words. Write sentences using each word.

Word Wise

Prefixes *im-* and *in-*

You will need

15 min.

- Teacher-made word cards
- paper
- pencils

● Choose five word cards from those provided by your teacher. Write your words in a list. Write sentences using each word. Think of other words with prefixes *im-* and *in-*. Add them to the list.

▲ Choose seven word cards from those provided by your teacher, and write the words in a list. Write a sentence using each word. Add other words with prefixes *im-* and *in-* to the list.

■ Choose ten words with prefizes *im-* and *in-* from those provided by your teacher and write your words in a list. Write sentences using each word. Think of other words with these prefixes. Write sentences using them.

Word Wise

Short Vowels; Syllables VC/CV

15 min.

You will need

- Teacher-made word cards
- paper
- pencils
- Letter Tiles

● Choose eight word cards from those provided by your teacher. Use the Letter Tiles to spell the words. Write sentences using five of the words.

▲ Choose eight word cards from those provided by your teacher. Use the Letter Tiles to spell the words. Write sentences using all of the words.

■ Choose ten word cards from those provided by your teacher. Write the words. Write sentences using each of your words.

Word Wise

Final Syllables -*tion*, -*ion*, -*ture*, -*ive*, -*ize*

15 min.

You will need
- Teacher-made word cards
- paper
- pencils

● Choose five word cards from those provided by your teacher. List your words. Write a sentence for each word. Add other words with final syllables -*tion*, -*ion*, -*ture*, -*ive*, -*ize* to your list.

▲ Choose eight word cards from those provided by your teacher and write your words in a list. Write a sentence for each word. Add other words with final syllables -*tion*, -*ion*, -*ture*, -*ive*, -*ize* to your list.

■ Choose ten word cards from those provided by your teacher and write your words in a list. Write sentences using each word. Add other words with these final syllables to your list.

Word Wise

Plurals with -s, -es, and -ies

15 min.

You will need
- Teacher-made word cards
- paper
- pencils

● Choose six word cards from those provided by your teacher. Write the words in a list. Circle the letters that make each word plural. Write sentences using four of the words.

▲ Choose ten word cards from those provided by your teacher and write the words. Circle the letters that make each word plural. Write sentences using six of the words.

■ Choose ten word cards from those provided by your teacher and write the words. Circle the letters that make each word plural. Write sentences using each of the words.

Word Wise

Schwa Sound Spelled with a, e, i, o, u, and y

You will need

15 min.

- Teacher-made word cards
- paper
- pencils

● Choose five word cards from those provided by your teacher. Write your words in a list. Write sentences using each word. List other words with the schwa sound spelled with *a, e, i, o, u,* or *y.*

▲ Choose seven word cards from those provided by your teacher. Write your words in a list. List other words with the schwa sound spelled with *a, e, i, o, u,* or *y,* and add them to your list. Write sentences for each of word.

■ Choose nine word cards from those provided by your teacher. Write your words in a list, and write a sentence for each. List other words with the schwa sound spelled with *a, e, i, o, u,* or *y.*

Word Wise

Endings -ed, -ing, -er, and -est

15 min.

You will need
- Teacher-made word cards
- paper
- pencils

● Choose four word cards from those provided by your teacher. Write the words in a list. Write sentences using each of your words. Add other words with these endings to your list.

▲ Choose six word cards from those provided by your teacher and write the words. Circle the *-ed, -ing, -er,* or *-est* ending that has been added to each base word. Write sentences using each of the words.

■ Choose nine word cards from those provided by your teacher and write the words in a list. Circle the ending that has been added to each base word. Write sentences using each of the words.

Word Wise

Vowel Sounds in *Moon* and *Foot*

You will need
15 min.

- Teacher-made word cards
- paper
- pencils

● Choose five word cards from those provided by your teacher. List your words. Write sentences using each word. List other words with the vowel sounds in *moon* and *foot* (*oo, ew, ue, ui,* and *oo, u*).

▲ Choose seven word cards from those provided by your teacher. List your words. Write sentences using each word. List other words with the vowel sounds in *moon* and *foot* (*oo, ew, ue, ui,* and *oo, u*).

■ Choose nine word cards from those provided by your teacher and write your words in a list. Write sentences using each word. Add other words with these vowel sounds.

Word Wise

Vowel Digraphs *ee, ea, ai, ay, oa,* and *ow*

15 min.

You will need
- Teacher-made word cards
- paper
- pencils

● Choose four word cards from those provided by your teacher. Write your words. Circle the two letters that form the long-vowel sound in each word. Write sentences using your words.

▲ Choose six word cards from those provided by your teacher and write your words. Circle the letters that form the long-vowel sound in each word. Write sentences using your words.

■ Choose eight word cards from those provided by your teacher and write your words. Circle the letters that form each long-vowel sound. Write sentences using your words. Add other words with similar spellings.

Word Wise

Suffixes -y, -ish, -hood, -ment

You will need

15 min.

- Teacher-made word cards • paper • pencils

● Choose five word cards from those provided by your teacher. List the words. Write sentences using each word. Think of other words with suffixes *-y, -ish, -hood,* and *-ment.* Add them to the list.

▲ Choose seven word cards from those provided by your teacher, and write them in a list. Write sentences using each word. Add other words with suffixes *-y, -ish, -hood,* and *-ment* to the list.

■ Choose nine word cards from those provided by your teacher, and list the words. Write sentences using each word. Think of other words with suffixes *-y, -ish, -hood,* and *-ment.* Add them to the list.

Word Wise

Vowel Dipthongs /ou/, /oi/

15 min.

You will need

- Letter Tiles
- paper
- pencils
- Teacher-made word cards

● Choose six word cards from those provided by your teacher. Make a two-column chart with the headings */ou/ Sound* and */oi/ Sound*. Write the words in the correct column. Use the Letter Tiles to spell each word.

▲ Choose six word cards from those provided by your teacher. Make a two-column chart with the headings */ou/ Sound* and */oi/ Sound*. Write the words in the correct column. Write sentences using three of your words.

■ Choose ten word cards from those provided by your teacher. Make a two-column chart with the headings */ou/ Sound* and */oi/ Sound*. Write the words in the correct column. Write sentences using three words with each sound.

Vowel Patterns *ei, eigh*

15 min.

You will need
- Teacher-made word cards
- paper
- pencils

● Choose five word cards from those provided by your teacher. Write the words. Write sentences using each word. Think of other words you know with vowel patterns *ei* and *eigh*. Add these words to the list.

▲ Choose seven word cards from those provided by your teacher, and list the words. Write sentences using each word. Think of other words you know with vowel patterns *ei* and *eigh*. Add the words to the list.

■ Choose nine word cards from those provided by your teacher and list the words. Write sentences for each word. Think of other words you know with vowel patterns *ei* and *eigh*, and add the words to the list.

Word Wise

Words V/VC and VC/V

15 min.

You will need
- Teacher-made word cards
- Letter Tiles
- paper
- pencils

● Choose six word cards from those provided by your teacher. Use the Letter Tiles to spell each word. Write sentences using three of your words.

▲ Choose eight word cards from those provided by your teacher and use the Letter Tiles to spell each word. Write sentences using five of your words.

■ Choose eight word cards from those provided by your teacher and write a list of your words. Write a sentence for each of your words.

Word Wise

Vowel Patterns *a, au, aw, al, augh, ough*

You will need

- Teacher-made word cards
- paper
- pencils

15 min.

● Choose five word cards from those provided by your teacher. Write the words. Underline the vowel pattern. Add other words you know with vowel patterns *a, au, aw, al, augh,* and *ough* to your list.

▲ Choose seven word cards from those provided by your teacher, and list your words. Write sentences using each of your words. Add other words you know with vowel patterns *a, au, aw, al, augh,* and *ough* to your list.

■ Choose nine word cards from those provided by your teacher, and write the words. Write sentences using each of the words. Think of other words with vowel patterns *a, au, aw, al, augh, ough.* Add them to your list.

Word Wise

Final Syllable -le

15 min.

You will need
- Teacher-made word cards
- Letter Tiles
- paper
- pencils

● Choose four word cards from those provided by your teacher. Use the Letter Tiles to spell each word. Write the words. Write sentences using each of the words.

▲ Choose six word cards from those provided by your teacher and use the Letter Tiles to spell each word. Write the words and then write sentences for six of the words.

■ Choose eight word cards from those provided by your teacher and write your words. Write sentences using each word. Think of other words you know with final syllable -le. Add the words to your list.

Homophones

You will need

15 min.

- Teacher-made word cards
- paper
- pencil

● Choose three pairs of homophones from the word cards from those provided by your teacher. Write the homophones side by side. Write sentences for each pair of homophones to show their different meanings.

▲ Choose four pairs of homophones from the word cards from those provided by your teacher. Write the homophones side by side. Write sentences for each pair of homophones to show their different meanings.

■ Choose five word cards from those provided by your teacher that do not sound alike. Write the words, and next to each word write a homophone. Write sentences for each pair to show their different meanings.

Word Wise

Compound Words

15 min.

You will need
- Teacher-made word cards
- paper
- pencil

● Choose five word cards from those provided by your teacher. Write your words. Next to each word write the two words that form the compound word. Write sentences using three of your compound words.

▲ Choose six word cards from those provided by your teacher. Write your words in a list. Next to each word write the two words that form the compound word. Write sentences using your compound words.

■ Choose eight word cards from those provided by your teacher. Write your words in a list. Next to each word write the two words that form the compound word. Write sentences using your compound words. List other compound words you know.

Word Wise

Syllable Pattern CV/VC

You will need

15 min.

- Teacher-made word cards
- paper
- pencil

● Choose five word cards from those provided by your teacher. Write the words. Draw slashes through words to break them into syllables. Write sentences using each word.

▲ Choose seven word cards from those provided by your teacher and write them. Draw slashes through the words to break them into syllables. Write sentences using each word.

■ Choose nine word cards from those provided by your teacher and write the words. Draw slashes through the words to break them into syllables. List each word's part of speech. Write sentences using each word.

Word Wise

Consonant Blends *squ, spl, thr,* and *str*

15 min.

Materials

- Teacher-made word cards
- paper
- pencil

● Choose five word cards from those provided by your teacher. Write your words. Write sentences using each word. List other words you know with *squ, spl, thr,* and *str*.

▲ Choose eight word cards from those provided by your teacher and write your words. Write sentences using six words. Add other words you know with *squ, spl, thr,* and *str* to your list.

■ Choose eight word cards from those provided by your teacher and write your words in a list. Write sentences using each word. Think of other words with *squ, spl, thr,* and *str* and add them to your list.

Word Wise

VCCV Spelling Pattern

You will need

15 min.

- Teacher-made word cards
- paper
- pencils

● Choose five word cards from those provided by your teacher. Write your words. Write sentences using each word. Write other words you know with the spelling pattern of three consonants between two vowels.

▲ Choose eight word cards from those provided by your teacher and write the words. Write sentences using each of the words. Write other words you know with the spelling pattern of three consonants between two vowels.

■ Choose ten word cards from those provided by your teacher and write the words. Write sentences using each word. Think of other words you know with VCCV spelling pattern and add them to your list.

Word Wise

Consonant Digraphs /sh/, /th/, /ch/, /ng/

You will need

15 min.

- Teacher-made word cards
- paper
- pencils

● Choose word cards from those provided by your teacher until you have one with each spelling: /sh/, /th/, /ch/, and /ng/. List your words. Write a sentence using each word. List other words with these spellings.

▲ Choose word cards from those provided by your teacher until you have two with each spelling: /sh/, /th/, /ch/, and /ng/. List your words. Write a sentence using each word. List other words with these spellings.

■ Choose word cards from those provided by your teacher until you have three with each spelling: /sh/, /th/, /ch/, and /ng/. List your words. Write a sentence using each word. List other words with these spellings.

Word Wise

Suffixes *-er*, *-or*, *-ess*, and *-ist*

15 min.

You will need

- Teacher-made word cards
- dictionary
- paper
- pencils

● Choose ten word cards from those provided by your teacher. Make a four-column chart. Use *-er*, *-or*, *-ess*, and *-ist* as headings. Write your words in the correct column. Write sentences with one word from each column.

▲ Choose twelve word cards from those provided by your teacher. Make a four-column chart with *-er*, *-or*, *-ess*, and *-ist* as headings. List each word in the correct column. Write sentences using two words from each column.

■ Choose fifteen word cards from those provided by your teacher and use *-er*, *-or*, *-ess*, and *-ist* as headings in a four-column chart. List the words in the columns. Write sentences using three words from each column.

Word Wise

Contractions

15 min.

You will need

- Teacher-made word cards
- paper
- pencils

● Choose five word cards from those provided by your teacher. Write your words in a list. Next to each word write the two words that form it. Write sentences using each contraction.

▲ Choose seven word cards from those provided by your teacher. Write the words in a list. Next to each word write the two words that form it. Write sentences using each of your contraction.

■ Choose nine word cards from those provided by your teacher and write your words in a list. Write the two words that form each contraction. Write sentences using each contraction. Add other contractions to the list.

Word Wise

Prefixes *pre-*, *mid-*, *over-*, *out-*, *bi-*, and *de-*

15 min.

You will need

- Teacher-made word cards
- dictionary
- paper
- pencils

● Choose word cards from those provided by your teacher until you have one each with *pre-*, *mid-*, *over-*, *out-*, *bi-*, and *de-*. Write the words in a list. Write sentences using words. Circle the prefix in each word.

▲ Choose word cards from those provided by your teacher until you have two with each prefix: *pre-*, *mid-*, *over-*, *out-*, *bi-*, and *de-*. Write the words. Write sentences using them. Circle the prefix in each word.

■ Choose word cards from those provided by your teacher until you have two with each prefix: *pre-*, *mid-*, *over-*, *out-*, *bi-*, and *de-*. List the words and write sentences using them. Add other words with these prefixes to your list.

Word Wise

Prefixes *un-, re-, mis-, dis-,* and *non-*

You will need

15 min.

- Teacher-made word cards   • paper   • pencils

● Find one word card from those provided by your teacher with each prefix: *un-, re-, mis-, dis-,* and *non-*. Write the words in a list. Circle the prefix in each word. Write sentences using your words.

▲ Find two word cards from those provided by your teacher with each prefix: *un-, re-, mis-, dis-,* and *non-*. List the words and circle each prefix. Write sentences using each word.

■ Choose three word cards from those provided by your teacher with each prefix: *un-, re-, mis-, dis-,* and *non-*. List the words. Write sentences using each word. Add words to your list.

Word Wise

r-Controlled Vowels

You will need

15 min.

- Teacher-made word cards
- paper
- pencil

● Choose five word cards from those provided by your teacher. Write your words in a list. Write sentences using each of your words. Think of other words you know with similar spellings. Add the words to your list.

▲ Choose seven word cards from those provided by your teacher and write your words in a list. Write a sentence for each of your words. Think of words you know with similar spellings and add them to your list.

■ Choose nine word cards from those provided by your teacher and write your words in a list. Write sentences using each of your words. List two more words with similar spelling patterns for every word on your list.

Word Wise

Spellings of /j/, /s/, /k/

15 min.

You will need
- Teacher-made word cards
- paper
- pencils

● Choose five word cards from those provided by your teacher. Write your words in a list. Write a sentence for each of the words. Think of other words you know with similar spellings. Add them to your list.

▲ Choose seven word cards from those provided by your teacher and write the words. Write a sentence for each of the words. Think of other words you know with similar spellings and add them to your list.

■ Choose nine word cards from those provided by your teacher and write the words. Write sentences using each of the words. Think of other words you know with similar spellings and add them to your list.

Word Wise

Irregular Plurals

15 min.

You will need
- paper
- pencil

● Choose four word cards from those provided by your teacher. Write the words. Write a sentence for each word. Next, write the singular form of each word. Add other irregular plurals you know to your list.

▲ Choose six word cards from those provided by your teacher and write the words. Write a sentence for each word. Write each word's singular form. Add other irregular plurals you know to your list.

■ Choose eight word cards from those provided by your teacher. Write the words and then write sentences for them. Write each word's singular form. Add other irregular plurals you know to your list.

Word Wise

Suffixes *-ly, -ful, -ness, -less, -able,* and *-ible*

15 min.

You will need

- Teacher-made word cards   • paper   • pencils

● Choose four word cards from those provided by your teacher. Write your words in a list. Write a sentence for each of the words. Add other words you know with the suffixes *-ly, -ful, -ness, -less, -able,* and *-ible* to your list.

▲ Choose six word cards from those provided by your teacher. Write your words in a list. Write a sentence for each of the words. Add other words you know with suffixes spelled *-ly, -ful, -ness, -less, -able,* and *-ible* to your list.

■ Choose eight word cards from those provided by your teacher and write the words. Write a sentence for each of the words. Add other words you know with these suffixes to your list.

Word Wise

Consonant Patterns *wr, kn, gn, st,* and *mb*

15 min.

You will need
- Teacher-made word cards
- paper
- pencil

● Choose at least one word card from those provided by your teacher with *wr, kn, gn, st,* and *mb*. Write sentences using each of the different spelling patterns. List other words you know with spelling patterns *wr, kn, gn, st,* and *mb*.

▲ Choose at least two word cards from those provided by your teacher with *wr, kn, gn, st,* and *mb*. Write two sentences using words with each different spelling pattern. List other words you know with these spellings.

■ Choose at least three word cards from those provided by your teacher with *wr, kn, gn, st,* and *mb*. Write three sentences using each spelling pattern. List other words with these spellings.